Pride

words&pictures

© 2025 Quarto Publishing Group USA Inc.
Illustrations © Amy Phelps 2025

First published in 2025 by words & pictures,
an imprint of The Quarto Group.
100 Cummings Center,
Suite 265D Beverly,
MA 01915, USA.
T (978) 282-9590 F (978) 283-2742
www.quarto.com

Editor: Alice Hobbs
Assistant Editor: Jackie Lui
Designers: Clare Barber and Mike Henson
Associate Publisher: Holly Willsher

ISBN: 978-1-8360-0087-7

9 8 7 6 5 4 3 2 1

Manufactured in Malaysia PCA 012025

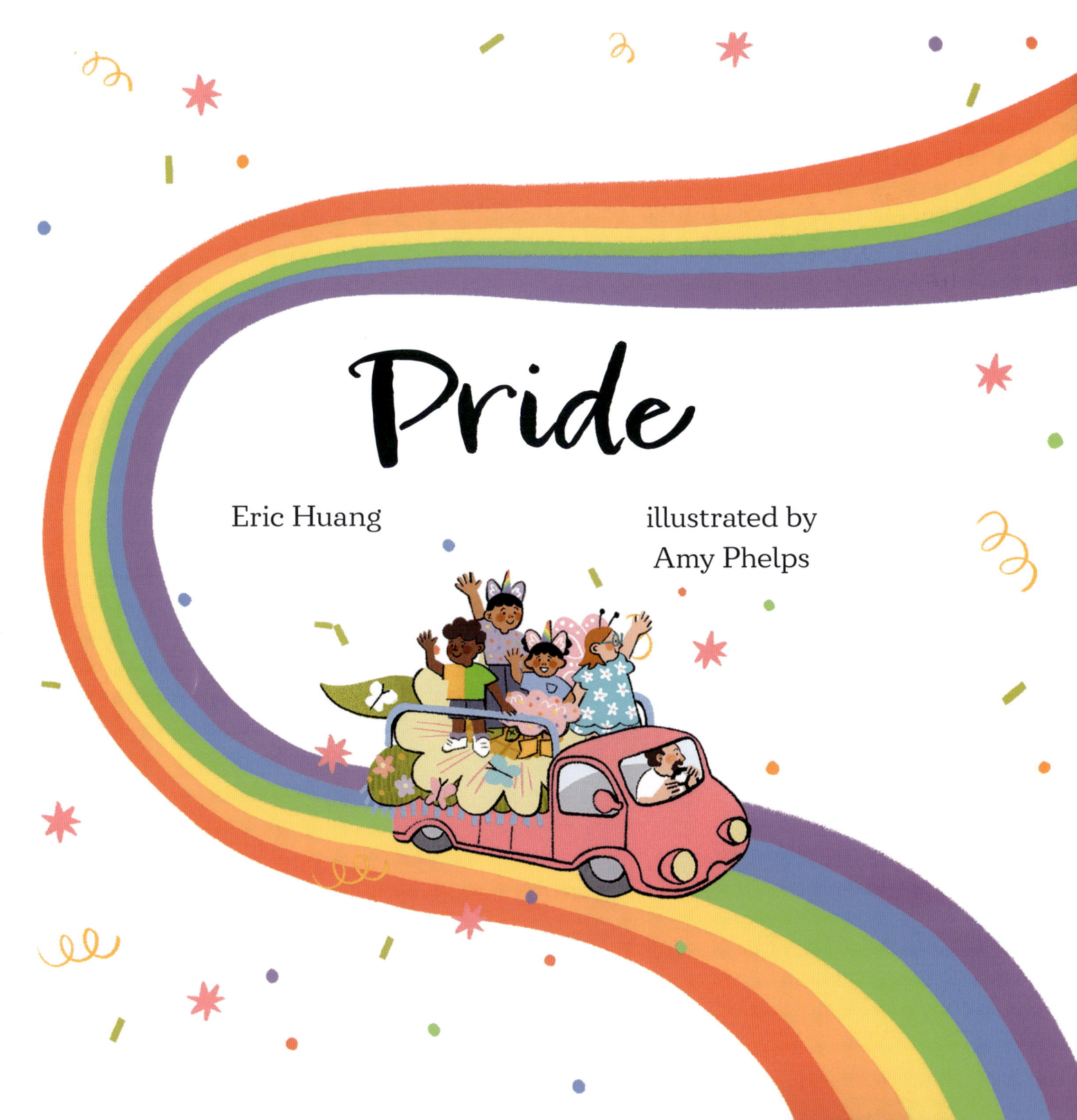

Pride

Eric Huang

illustrated by
Amy Phelps

Happy Pride Month!

My name is Brian. These are my dads.
They are taking me to a parade this weekend.
The Pride parade! It's a fun-filled day with
music, dancing, and colorful floats in
celebration of LGBTQIA+ people.

Everyone's welcome!

My best friends David, Nicola, and Charlie are coming too. Our families will celebrate together. But first, we need to decide what to wear . . .

5

At school we're learning about how Pride Month started. Our teacher, Ms. Macleod, describes a historic protest called the Stonewall Uprising. We learn that it happened at the Stonewall Inn in New York City. There were lots of speeches and marches for weeks afterward.

Nicola asks Ms. Macleod about the signs people carried in the march.

"They're all homemade messages in support of equality," Ms. Macleod says.

We spend the rest of the lesson making our own signs to take to the Pride parade this weekend.

Ms. Macleod makes sure we learn about LGBTQIA+ rights throughout the year. Last October it was LGBTQ+ History Month.

8

We learned about the lives of many brave people who fought for equality—and people who are still standing up against unfair treatment today.

Josephine Baker

Gus Kenworthy

There are so many famous queer people, from artists to athletes, singers to scientists—and even kings and queens! I was happy to learn that there have always been amazing people just like my dads.

During Pride Month there are lots of fun events. At lunchtime, Charlie and David tell us about a Pride event they attended last weekend. It was a Pride trail at the museum.

David and Charlie were given checklists with ten Pride-related things to look for. They got stickers for each one they found. When they had spotted all ten, they traded in the checklist for a cookie at the museum café.

Afterward, David and Charlie made paintings inspired by the work of a queer artist.

There are so many fun things to do during Pride Month. Nicola tells us about the Pride crafting day her parents took her to at the weekend.

"We made Pride bracelets," Nicola says. She shows us the colorful bracelet on her arm, then reaches into her backpack.

"I made these for you!" Nicola gives each of us our very own Pride bracelet. We decide to wear them at the Pride parade.

After school we go to
Charlie and David's house.
Their parents show us
pictures from past Pride
parades. We're hoping to get
ideas for what to wear.

They wore a lot of very skinny
jeans! But I still don't know
what I want to wear.

After some snacks, we walk to the library. A drag queen story hour is starting soon. Miss Paige Turner reads a book about a rainbow unicorn named Giggles Glitterhorn.

Charlie and David decide they're both going to be rainbow unicorns for the Pride parade.

After school the next day, Nicola's mom and dad drive us into town. We're helping make a Pride float for an LGBTQIA+ charity.

It's going to be a giant flower surrounded by butterflies. We cut out pink, light-blue, and white butterflies to decorate the float. Nicola's mom tells us these colors represent the transgender community.

Nicola decides she's going to attend the parade wearing butterfly wings, dressed in pink, light-blue, and white!

When I get home from making the float, I'm a little sad. My dads ask me what's wrong.

"I don't know what I want to wear to the Pride parade," I tell them.

"It doesn't matter what you wear, Brian," they reply. "What's important is that you're at the parade to show your support—and have fun."

My dads help me try
on a few different
outfits. None of them
are quite right . . .

19

I can't concentrate at school on Friday. I still haven't figured out what to wear to the Pride parade.

"Be a rainbow unicorn and join our herd!" Charlie suggests.

"Fly with me as a butterfly!" Nicola says.

David thinks I should be a sparkly cowboy.

After school, I sit with my dads at the kitchen table. We're making Pride flags together to take to the parade. I use glitter to make my rainbow flag really shiny. My dads use lots of different colors for their flags.

That night, my dads and I host a pizza party. Everyone has a lot of fun.

"We're one big happy family," Uncle Bruno says. I remind Uncle Bruno that I'm not related to any of the guests except for him.

"You don't have to be related to be family," Uncle Bruno explains. "We're a chosen family— like different colors, coming together to make a rainbow!"

That gives me an idea . . .

When the guests leave, I gather all my art supplies and get to work.

23

The Pride parade is today! I am so excited.

Nicola, Charlie, and David come over for lunch with their parents. Everyone shows off their outfits.

Nicola's dad baked a rainbow Pride cake. We each have a slice and dance around the kitchen.

"Is that your Pride parade outfit?" Nicola asks. I'm wearing a T-shirt I made last night.

"I like the colors!" Charlie says.

David asks, "But what does it mean?"

"You'll see!" I tell them.

25

After a few minutes, my dads
join us in the kitchen.
They've changed into the Pride
T-shirts I made for them.

When we stand together,
we're a rainbow.

My dads have a surprise for me too.
It's a colorful hat! They tell me how the
colors and shapes represent different
members of our queer family.

Now we're all ready
to join the parade!

There are lots of people in town. Some have even brought their pets. Charlie, David, Nicola, and I count them all. Look at that wiener dog wearing a rainbow hoodie!

The whole town is decorated for the parade. Our local bookshop has a display of LGBTQIA+ books in the window. A rainbow flag waves from a flagpole at the library. The donut shop even has special rainbow donuts. Yum!

We join the parade riding on our butterfly float. Firefighters march behind us. In front, a group of motorcyclists lead the way. We dance on the float and wave at all of the people who have come to cheer.

One of the firefighters gives his hat to Nicola!

At the end of the parade there's a big concert and lots of food. My dads love the singers performing. We all dance and sing.

I have the best time with my chosen family.

31

I smile whenever I think about Pride Month. Our town looks so cool covered in rainbows.

Even though Pride Month is over, there are queer events almost every week. Anyone can celebrate Pride throughout the year!

I'm already looking forward to next year's Pride parade. But there's something else on my mind, too . . .

What am I going to wear?

The Stonewall Uprising

Pride Month is a celebration of LGBTQIA+ people, culture, and history. It's also a commemoration of a historic protest called the Stonewall Uprising.

The protest was held on June 28, 1969 at the Stonewall Inn in New York City. Afterward, there were weeks of demonstrations to demand equality for queer people.

UNITED STATES—JUNE 28: Stonewall Inn nightclub raid. Crowd attempts to stop police arrests outside the Stonewall Inn on Christopher Street in Greenwich Village.

Many people were involved in the Stonewall Uprising. Three key activists were Marsha P. Johnson, Sylvia Rivera, and Stormé DeLarverie. All three fought for equality throughout their lives and had a significant impact on LGBTQIA+ history and culture.

Many speeches and marches took place at Christopher Park, which is just across the street from the inn. Together, the park and the inn became the Stonewall National Monument in 2016.

Marsha P. Johnson

Today, Pride is a month-long celebration—but it began as a protest for equal rights!

THE FIGHT FOR EQUALITY

The Stonewall Uprising wasn't the first LGBTQIA+ protest, but it's the most famous one. Here are some early protests in the United States that paved the way for Stonewall and future demonstrations around the world.

Cooper Do-nuts Riot, **Los Angeles**, 1958

Black Nite Brawl, **Milwaukee**, 1961

Dewey's Sit-In, **Philadelphia**, 1965

Julius Tavern Sip-In, **New York City**, 1966

Compton's Cafeteria Riot, **San Francisco**, 1966

Black Cat Tavern Protests, **Los Angeles**, 1966-67

The Gay Liberation Monument, created by George Segal

Sylvia Rivera

Stormé DeLarverie

LGBTQIA+

LGBTQIA+ stands for: lesbian, gay, bisexual, trans, queer/questioning, intersex, and asexual/aromantic/agender. Some say the "A" also stands for "ally." The "+" is included to represent all the other sexualities and gender identities which aren't included in these letters.

The First Pride Month

In 1970, a year after the Stonewall Uprising, Pride marches were held in New York City, Los Angeles, and Chicago on June 28 to remember the event. This was the first Pride Month.

The effects of the Stonewall Uprising weren't only felt in the United States. The first ever Pride march in the UK was also inspired by this historic protest. The march was held on July 1, 1972, on the Saturday closest to the anniversary of the uprising.

Since then, Pride parades and Pride Month events have been organized all over the world. Many happen in June, but celebrations occur somewhere in the world every month of the year!

FEBRUARY
Auckland Pride, **New Zealand**
Mumbai Pride, **India**

JANUARY
Whistler Gay Ski Week, **Canada**
Midsumma Festival, **Australia**

DECEMBER
Pink Christmas, **Germany**
Holly Folly, **MA, U.S.**

NOVEMBER
Hong Kong Pride, **Hong Kong**
Buenos Aires Pride, **Argentina**

OCTOBER
Johannesburg Pride, **South Africa**
West Hollywood Halloween Carnaval, **CA, U.S.**

SEPTEMBER
Pride Belgrade, **Serbia**
Benidorm Pride, **Spain**

MARCH
European Snow Pride, **France**

Sydney Mardi Gras, **Australia**

APRIL
Tokyo Rainbow Pride, **Japan**

Phuket Gay Pride, **Thailand**

MAY
Cyprus Pride Festival, **Cyprus**

Sao Paulo Trans+ Pride, **Brazil**

JUNE
Pride Puerto Rico, **Puerto Rico**

Baltic Pride, **Estonia**

JULY
Manuel Antonio Pride, **Costa Rica**

London Trans+ Pride, **UK**

AUGUST
Amsterdam Pride, **Netherlands**

XLSIOR Mykonos, **Greece**

PRIDE CELEBRATIONS AROUND THE WORLD

Pride Month events around the globe include diverse traditions and customs. Many people celebrating Pride in Texas wear cowboy hats. Some who march in the Rainbow Pride parade in Tokyo dress up in traditional Japanese kimonos. And the Pride festivals in Mexico feature Indigenous music and dance.

Here's a calendar showing just a handful of Pride events around the world.

LGBTQ+ History Month

While many events fill the days of Pride Month, there's a separate month dedicated to LGBTQIA+ history. The first LGBTQ+ History Month was in October 1994. It was started by a high-school history teacher in Missouri named Rodney Wilson.

Wilson was inspired by two events in October to transform the entire month into an LGBTQIA+ celebration:

October 11, NATIONAL COMING OUT DAY: This is a day that raises awareness of LGBTQIA+ experiences. It's also an international celebration that urges everyone to embrace their identity and the diversity of the queer community.

October 14, ANNIVERSARY OF THE NATIONAL MARCH ON WASHINGTON FOR LESBIAN AND GAY RIGHTS: On this day in 1979, about 100,000 people marched in the U.S. capital to demand laws to protect the rights of LGBTQIA+ people.

Visit your local library to find out about the LGBTQ+ History Month events in your neighborhood!

In the UK, LGBT+ History Month is February. It was founded by education charity Schools OUT and was first celebrated in 2005. February was chosen to mark the anniversary of a discriminatory law called Section 28 finally being overturned in 2003. Later, a law called the Equality Act was brought in to protect people from discrimination based on their sexual orientation, religion, gender, or age.

Schools, libraries, museums, and more all hold LGBT+ History Month events throughout the month to highlight important events and people in the ongoing fight for equality.

LGBTQIA+ HISTORY AROUND THE WORLD

Hungary has held LGBTQ+ History Month celebrations since 2013. Events range from exhibitions about queer athletes to film screenings.

In **Germany**, Queer History Month is celebrated in May in the city of Berlin. The city's many museums run themed tours during the month to tell the stories of the queer artists, musicians, writers, and others who have called the city home.

The annual LGBTQ+ Cuba History Month is also in May and features a big Pride parade. **Cuba** is the first Latin American country to hold a month dedicated to queer history!

Australia celebrates Australian LGBTQ+ History Month in October, with National Coming Out Day on the 11th at the center of the festivities. The first celebration was held in 2016.

The Pride Flag

The rainbow Pride flag was designed in 1978 by an artist named Gilbert Baker. He and 30 volunteers created two flags. They flew above the San Francisco Civic Center on July 25, 1978, the date of San Francisco's Pride celebration and parade.

The first Pride flag had eight colors. The modern design is simpler, with six colors forming a rainbow. Each color has a meaning.

The rainbow flag pattern is used in many different ways. You can see it on crosswalks, on the sides of buses, on cups, cupcakes, T-shirts, and even on hoodies for pets!

Together the colors represent diversity.

RED = LIFE

ORANGE = HEALING

YELLOW = SUNLIGHT

GREEN = NATURE

BLUE = SERENITY

PURPLE = SPIRIT

The Intersex-Inclusive Flag, also known as the Progress Pride flag, represents everyone in the queer community.

INTERSEX-INCLUSIVE FLAG

This flag is one of the most recent and most inclusive Pride flags. It was designed by Valentino Vecchietti in 2021 and celebrates the diversity of the LGBTQIA+ community.

The purple circle on a yellow background represents intersex people. The white, pink, and blue stripes are from the Transgender Pride Flag. The brown and black stripes reference the Philadelphia Pride Flag created in 2017 to recognize queer people of color.

Make a Pride Flag

Make a rainbow Pride flag that celebrates your family!

MATERIALS

- Letter-sized cardstock
- Letter-sized colored construction paper, one sheet each in red, orange, yellow, green, blue, and purple
- White letter-size paper
- Crayons, markers, colored pencils, or paint
- Stickers
- Glue
- Scissors

CREATE A RAINBOW

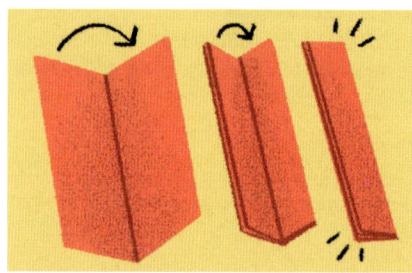

1. Fold a piece of colored construction paper in half, lengthwise, three times.

2. Open the folded paper and cut along the folds to make six strips.

3. Repeat with the five remaining pieces of colored construction paper so that you have six strips of each color.

4. Glue one strip of each color horizontally onto the cardstock to cover it in a rainbow pattern. Start with a red strip at the top, then orange, yellow, green, blue, and finally, purple. You can also make your own color pattern!

5. If you don't have construction paper, use crayons, markers, colored pencils, or paint to draw bands of color onto the cardstock.

ADD YOUR FAMILY

6. Draw pictures of your family members onto the white paper. Color them in if you like. Remember that your chosen family can include friends—and even pets!

7. Cut out the drawings of your family.

8. Use glue to stick the drawings onto the rainbow flag.

DECORATE THE FLAG

9. Decorate the flag with more drawings or stickers.

10. You might want to add hearts, smaller rainbows, unicorns, or butterflies.

11. You can also write messages on pieces of paper, and glue them onto the flag.

You can use the leftover strips of paper to make more colorful flags for your friends and family. Display the Pride flag in a window—or bring it with you to a Pride parade!

43

Baking Rainbow Pride Cookies

Make these rainbow Pride cookies for a Pride parade snack!

> Always ask an adult to help when using an oven!

INGREDIENTS

- 1 cup unsalted butter (or vegan butter)
- ⅔ cup caster sugar
- 2 cups all-purpose flour
- 1 teaspoon vanilla extract
- Rainbow sprinkles and/or colored icing

INSTRUCTIONS

1. Preheat the oven to 325°F.

2. Use a mixer or mixing spoon to combine the butter and sugar.

3. Mix in the flour and vanilla until it forms a light dough.

4. Roll a lump of dough into a ball about an inch wide.

5. Place the ball onto a baking sheet lined with baking paper, then use the palm of your hand to flatten the dough into a circle.

6. If you're using rainbow sprinkles, place some sprinkles on the flattened dough and press them in.

7. Repeat with the rest of the dough, making sure you leave about an inch between each circle.

8. Bake for 15 minutes.

9. Ask and adult to take out the baking sheet and let the cookies cool for at least 15 minutes.

10. If you're using colored icing, decorate the cooled cookies with rainbow patterns, as shown.

Enjoy the rainbow Pride cookies. Share them with your friends and family!

45

Families say PRIDE!

Quiz

How much do you know about Pride?
Take this quiz to find out!

1. When was the first Pride
Month in the United States?

2. What city did the Stonewall
Uprising take place in?

3. What does the color green
in the rainbow Pride flag stand for?

4. When is National Coming
Out Day celebrated?

5. What is the name of the park across
the street from the Stonewall Inn?

6. Which organization founded LGBT+
History Month in the UK?

7. Which of these colors isn't in the Intersex-Inclusive Pride Flag?
A. Pink   **C.** Orange
B. Gold   **D.** Blue

8. What did Nicola dress up as for the Pride parade?

9. What type of family includes people who aren't related to you?

10. Who designed the original rainbow Pride flag?

Proud, queer, and fabulous!

Marching for Pride!

Answers on the next page!

Answers

1. 1970

2. New York City

3. Nature

4. October 11

5. Christopher Park

6. Schools OUT

7. Gold

8. A butterfly

9. Chosen family

10. Gilbert Baker